# Summary:

# Principles

## By: Ray Dalio

Proudly Brought to you by:

## Legal & Disclaimer

# Table of Contents

# The Book at a Glance

How we live our lives greatly depend on the principles we've developed throughout its course. These principles serve as our guiding light whenever we're faced with obstacles, in order to achieve what our hearts desire.

Dalio is a respected financial expert who has lived through the toughest economic times and still managed to keep his life together. His secret to how he made it – his principles – are laid down in this book.

Principles by Ray Dalio is divided into 29 chapters categorized into three main parts. The first part of the book bolsters Dalio's credibility by providing readers with an overview of how Dalio lived his life. Chapter 1 shares Dalio's early years, depicting how he became interested in earning money and in the stock market. Chapter 2 narrates his college years, and how he started his business. In chapter 3, Dalio shares how his business suffered because of a mistake he made. Nonetheless, he shares how he was able to rebuild the business in chapter 4. In chapter 5, Dalio shares how the business grew and gained much recognition after overcoming the 2008 financial crisis. While in chapter 6, Dalio expressed his desire to step down from his position. Chapter 7 talks about Dalio's temporary transition plan. Part I concludes with chapter 8, where Dalio fondly looks back at his experiences which led to the discovery of his principles.

In Part II, Dalio shares life principles, which he developed through experience and reflection. Chapter 9 discusses why we should embrace reality and lays down the sub-principles to help us deal with it. Chapter 10 breaks down the 5-Step Process to help us get what we want out of life. To create a meaningful life, chapter 11 teaches us how we should be radically open-minded. Chapter 12 opens our minds to the fact that different people are wired differently. And finally, Dalio shares his secrets to making effective decisions in chapter 13.

Part III of this book is further sub-divided into three categories to help readers: get the culture right, get the people right, and build and evolve his business machine. Chapter 14 is about being open to knowing the truth and being honest with your colleagues. Chapter 15 lists the guidelines in order to cultivate meaningful work and relationships. Chapter 16 helps us realize that it's okay to make mistakes. Getting and staying in sync with our colleagues is at the heart of chapter 17. Dalio lays down the guidelines for weighing out our decisions in chapter 18. And finally, chapter 19 narrates the principles to guide us to go beyond disagreements.

The second sub-category of Part III begins with chapter 20, where Dalio emphasizes how important people are in running a business. Chapter 21 discusses the importance of hiring the right people. In chapter 22, Dalio lays emphasis on constantly training, testing, evaluating, and sorting people to ensure efficient output.

The third sub-category of Part III talks about how successful people build and evolve, and how their management machinery works. Chapter 23 teaches us that in order to achieve a goal, we must manage it as if we're operating a machine. In chapter 24, Dalio lists principles to keep us from tolerating our problems. On the other hand, chapter 25 describes ways to diagnose problems in order to resolve them effectively. Similarly, chapter 26 guides us in designing improvements to the machine so that it will work its way around problems. Chapter 27 reminds us to remain focused and do what we've set out to do. Dalio also shares the importance of using tools in protocols to get things done in chapter 28. And finally, chapter 29 emphasizes the importance of good governance.

This book is designed to help you respond to life's myriad of circumstances. Readers can expect that the main points of this book are neatly outlined so that they can easily distinguish between main principles, mid-principles, and sub-principles.

# FREE BONUSES

### P.S. Is it okay if we overdeliver?

Here at Readtrepreneur Publishing, we believe in overdelivering way beyond our reader's expectations. Is it okay if we overdeliver?

Here's the deal, we're going to give you an extremely condensed PDF summary of the book which you've just read and much more…

What's the catch? We need to trust you… You see, we want to overdeliver and in order for us to do that, we've to trust our reader to keep this bonus a secret to themselves? Why? Because we don't want people to be getting our exclusive PDF summaries even without buying our books itself. Unethical, right?

Ok. Are you ready?

Firstly, remember that your book is code: "**READ67**".

Next, visit this link: **http://bit.ly/exclusivepdfs**

Everything else will be self explanatory after you've visited: **http://bit.ly/exclusivepdfs**.

We hope you'll enjoy our free bonuses as much as we enjoyed preparing it for you!

# My Call to Adventure: 1949-1967

Ray Dalio was born in 1949 in a middle-class neighborhood in Long Island. He considered himself to be generally average, except for the fact that he didn't like going to school. He admits that he had poor grades because he didn't like what was being taught at school.

Nonetheless, Dalio proudly claims that if he was ever interested in something, then nothing would hold him back from doing it. At age eight, Dalio delivered newspapers, shoveled snow off people's driveways, and waited tables and washed dishes at a local restaurant. And from these jobs, he was able to learn things that aren't taught at school but are nonetheless helpful in day-to-day situations.

At twelve years old, Dalio worked as a caddy at the local golf course. He overheard players talking about putting their money in the stock market since the economy was looking good. At the time, the United States was both an economic and military powerhouse. This led Dalio to invest his savings in the stock market. And when his initial investment tripled, he became hooked.

By reading the free annual reports from a business magazine, Dalio expanded his knowledge about the stock market. These reports led him to discover the various investment strategies, and which one was frequently used by investors. He also became familiar with stocks, noting which ones are promising and avoiding those that aren't.

As a teenager, he enjoyed playing the market as much as he loved playing with his friends. In fact, he felt as though he was a normal teenage boy, except that he was knowledgeable about the stock market. At this point, he became an independent thinker who wasn't afraid of risks as long as something rewarding would result from it. He believed that "great" is better than "terrible", and that "terrible" is better than "mediocre" – because "terrible" adds flavor to one's life.

The year was 1966, and unknown to Ray Dalio, the stock market was at its peak when he was in senior year in high school. In just a couple of months, almost everything he thought he knew about markets would be proven wrong.

# Crossing the Threshold: 1967-1979

The economy went sour beginning in 1967. But as young as he was, Dalio remained optimistic and still kept buying stocks in the hope of a rebound. Unfortunately, it didn't happen. He lost money and watched the market fall during these years.

At around the same time, he also began going to college where he majored in finance. This time, he was doing well academically because it was a subject that he was genuinely interested in.

He also began to learn how to meditate. Dalio shares that his interest in meditation began when the Beatles visited India to study Transcendental Meditation. Fortunately, he was living in an era that was supportive of these mind-opening studies. According to Dalio, these times led them to open his mind and question the established ways of doing things.

Dalio also recalls that it was between these dates that young men were being drafted because of the Vietnam War. He observed how the country's politics and economy deteriorated, which in effect, caused the country's mood to become depressed. True enough, these were difficult years for the United States.

Since he was diagnosed with hypoglycemia, Ray Dalio was declared to be exempt from rendering military services. This gave him an opportunity to continue observing the economy. And true enough, he noticed that gold began to take over world markets around 1970 or 1971. This led him to realize that other currencies were fixed against the dollar, which, in turn, is also fixed against gold. Thus, he began to pay attention to the currency system.

Around 1971, he began working as a clerk on the floor of the New York Stock Exchange. Unfortunately, at that time, the dollar was facing a crisis and was about to reach a breaking point. It was also around this time that the dollar plummeted because President Nixon declared that the US Dollar would be fiat currency. The global monetary system was in chaos.

Nonetheless, Dalio observed that despite the declaration, the stock market regained its pace. At this point, he has already experienced so many events that led him to understand the cause-and-effect of market prices, and how politics and the economy would intertwine with each other.

At that time, he also became interested in commodities, which was unusual for a Harvard Business School (HBS)

4

student. Because of his interest in this venture, he eventually landed a job at Dominick & Dominick, a hundred-year-old brokerage firm, where he was appointed as director of commodities.

It was also around this time that Dalio set up a little business with his friends from HBS, which they called Bridgewater. He set up a bedroom in his apartment as his office, and hired an assistant. He would spend hours every day studying markets and trying to put himself in his clients' position because Bridgewater's goal was to help its clients beat the market.

Bridgewater helped Dalio gain a deeper understanding of how markets work. He was no longer limited to stocks and commodities – clients were pouring in from all around the world, and they had Dalio create business models for the livestock, meat, grain, and oilseed markets.

Dalio shares that the secret to his successful business was because of the fact that he didn't focus on making money. To him, it was of utmost importance that he had meaningful work, which led him to forge meaningful relationships. He kept in mind that while money is something we need in our daily lives, it certainly isn't the only thing we need.

# My Abyss: 1979-1982

At this stage in his life, Dalio observed yet another shift in the market. In previous decades, changes in the individual supply and demand were the main things that influenced the markets. During this time, however, he noted that markets began to move in unison – a result of swings in money, credit growth, and the oil shock.

This shift in the market's behavior led Dalio to study macroeconomics and historical data. At the same time, inflation plagued the economy, which led Dalio to predict that a catastrophic debt crisis would ensue.

To give us an idea of how bad the inflation spiral was at that time, Dalio shares the story of Bunker Hunt, who was then the richest man in the world. Bunker bought silver at around $1.29 per ounce as a security against inflation – and he kept doing so until it was at $10 per ounce. At this point, Dalio advised him that it's time to get out because he predicted that the economy would go down soon.

However, Bunker didn't heed Dalio's advice. He continued buying silver – which went as high as $50 per ounce. And the plunge did happen. On March 1980, silver went back to $11, which took Bunker down with it. The collapse of the world's richest man also caused a ripple effect, which greatly affected the U.S. economy.

From Bunker's experience, Dalio realized that his predictions were right. Nonetheless, timing is everything. He was fortunate enough to have gotten out of the silver roller coaster early on.

As the years progressed, the economy became worse. Between 1979 and 1982, debt was at its highest level – in fact, debt was at its highest since the Great Depression. Backed by his studies and calculations of debt since the 1800s, Dalio warned his clients of this depression. His view was seen as controversial, since people associated "depression" as something that had been sensationalized.

Nonetheless, Dalio was persistent in getting his theory through to people to save them from this economic decline. He challenged people to find flaws in his reasoning, which they failed to do. Eventually, he won them over.

True enough, timing was everything. In 1982, Mexico defaulted on its debt – a huge blow to U.S. banks that lent their capital to Mexico and similar countries. Since Dalio had predicted something like this would happen, he was invited to testify in a must-watch business show where he shared his prediction about the upcoming depression.

Unknown to Dalio, things were going to take a turn from that point on. The Fed responded to the economic collapse by making money readily available, and this caused the market to go into a bull run. Dalio publicly declared that this was merely a temporary solution. He was wrong – the inflation fell while the economy grew, which the U.S. enjoyed for the next eighteen years.

Dalio figured out why it all happened, but his being publicly wrong cost him too much. After eight years in business, he was back to square one. He lost too much money that he could no longer pay the people who worked with him, and Bridgewater was reduced from a booming enterprise to a one-man operation

Fortunately, being publicly wrong was a humbling experience for Dalio. He was also able to pick up lessons from these experiences, which he used as guiding principles throughout his life and work.

# My Road of Trials: 1983-1994

Dalio recalled that during this period, he was too broke to even go to Texas to meet with a prospective client. But being the persistent person that he is, Bridgewater was eventually back on its feet. He was able to maintain his upswings with tolerable downswings.

This was also the period when companies began investing in computers to make tasks easier, and Bridgewater was no exception. Dalio shares that he and his team programmed their computer to crunch statistics and economic data to arrive at an accurate economic prediction. Eventually, he realized that he could sell these data to consumers, thereby expanding the business to three main areas: financial and risk consulting, managing clients' risks, and selling research packages. This led Bridgewater to rise from the ashes and regain its former glory.

The resurrection of Bridgewater also opened many opportunities for Dalio. In 1984, he became interested in Beijing when he saw that there were no financial markets in China that time. Nonetheless, he foresaw that the country had the potential to become an economic powerhouse. And in 1994, Bridgewater China Partners was established.

Unfortunately, managing both Bridgewater and Bridgewater China Partners was too challenging, so he closed the latter after about a year in operation. Fortunately, no one lost any money. Dalio still thinks that if he had spent more time in managing China Partners, there was a big chance that it would become a success. Nonetheless, Dalio does not regret closing down China Partners – because if he didn't, Bridgewater would not be what it is today.

During this period, Bridgewater was already managing millions worth of funds, but they were still hell-bent on getting a larger foothold. The foothold they were looking for arrived in the form of Kodak's pension plan. As soon as they received the fax from Rusty Olson, CIO of Kodak's pension plan, asking for a solution to their investment problem, the Bridgewater team immediately leaped into action. And for Dalio and his team, this was more than bolstering their credibility – it was a complete game changer.

Dalio also shared that his team discovered the Holy Grail of investing during this period. According to this principle, having a few good uncorrelated return streams is better than having just one, and this became Bridgewater's key to investment success.

But if there is something that Dalio learned from all these experiences, it's this: mistakes happen all the time. Early on, he realized that mistakes should be seen as opportunities to learn and improve – and not as something to be ashamed of. True enough, the more people opened up about their mistakes, the more efficient they became as a team. In turn, they were able to find solutions to similar problems, which eventually helped them save on unnecessary expenses.

Another key to the success of Bridgewater lies in how the team would resolve their disagreements. To summarize, Dalio lays down the following guidelines in coming up with an agreement within an organization:

1. Be honest with your colleagues;

2. Disagree in a way that you can shape your opinions while learning at the same time; and

3. Have a means of settling the disagreement – like a vote – to help you go beyond the issue.

# The Ultimate Boon: 1995-2010

By 1995, Bridgewater became a well-equipped establishment with forty-two employees and $4.1 billion under management. Dalio points out that this was made possible through the company's digital system – which led him to hire young programmers and invest in more sophisticated computers.

Year after year, Dalio saw how Bridgewater grew into the investment powerhouse that it is today. In fact, statistics reveal that the amount the company has been managing grew almost eight times in just five years – reflective of how the public trusts Bridgewater. And as the business grew, it was inevitable for the company to blow up to become a full-sized institution.

However, the transition from being a boutique-sized investment management firm to a real institution was challenging. In fact, he was also facing a crisis of his own, because he was beginning to feel like he no longer had work-life balance. But by fleshing out the necessary principles, he was able to work things out with his managers and department heads. These work principles will be disclosed in succeeding chapters.

In 2007, the company's systems foresaw a bubble of debt, which could cause catastrophic damage to the economy. Out of fear of what previously happened to him between 1979 and 1982, Dalio consulted with several financial experts for their opinion on the matter. As it turned out, all of them foresaw the same thing – the financial and economic crisis of 2008.

Fortunately, they were successfully able to navigate through this tough period. While other investors reported losses of about 30 percent, the company's flagship fund increased by over 14 percent. And since the company successfully navigated through one of the biggest recorded crisis in U.S. history, more people became aware of it.

By 2010, the company had been making impressive returns, thanks to how well the systems were at taking in and processing information. In fact, statistics show that Bridgewater was able to make over 40 percent in 2010 alone. But at the same time, Dalio was already sixty years old and was preparing the company to succeed without him.

# Returning the Boon: 2011-2015

According to Dalio, life consists of three phases: being dependent on others while we learn, having others depend on us while we work, and the last is not having anyone depend on us, not having to work, and being free to enjoy life. During the period between 2011 and 2015, Dalio was already preparing for his transition from the second to the third phase of his life.

He knew that the transition would not be easy. At that time, he was responsible for two jobs at Bridgewater: as chief executive officer and as chief investment officer. For a long time, he pondered about whether he should completely leave management or stay as a mentor during the transition. If he stepped down, new leaders had the freedom to make their own decisions, but on the other hand, his constant fear of a turbulent transition made him think twice.

After much deliberation and inspiration from esteemed Singaporean leader Lee Kwan Yew, Dalio finally decided that he would stay as mentor. And in 2011, he announced that he would be stepping down as CEO.

Just like his prediction, the new management team did struggle after he stepped down. Thus, during this period, he made sure that his goal was to pass the knowledge he acquired from experiences – also known as "returning the boon". The reflections and principles he discussed with his team will be outlined in succeeding chapters.

It was also during this period that Dalio began his philanthropic journey. He shares that the experience of giving away his money to help a bigger purpose made him feel happy – he felt like it was the right thing to do at that stage of his life.

And in June 2015, Bridgewater turned forty years old. For a company that has been through so much in the last four decades, this was something that truly calls for a celebration.

# My Last Year and My Greatest Challenge: 2016-2017

Dalio considers this stage as his last year with Bridgewater. Although the investment aspect of the business was doing well, he felt as though the other aspects were slipping.

During this time, Dalio had already stepped down as CEO of the company, but was nonetheless tasked to oversee its current CEOs. Greg Jensen and Eileen Murray succeeded him. Even when they were both talented experts and experienced leaders, the leadership transition was still difficult.

Although leadership transitions are never easy, they managed to resolve disagreements through exchanging views and voting upon alternative paths. In March 2016, the result of the vote was out: Greg would step down and focus on being the co-chief investment officer, while Dalio would temporarily join Eileen as co-CEO to help with the transition.

Unfortunately, the media highly sensationalized this leadership move, which caused Greg and Dalio so much pain.

The stories they depicted were inaccurate portrayals of the company's disagreement resolution method. Fortunately, Greg took this painful experience and converted it into a learning experience, which helped him improve.

It was also an enlightening experience for Dalio. A friend of his, management expert Jim Collins, advised that a successful transition requires getting two things done: the first is having a capable CEO, and the second is having a capable governance system to replace CEOs if they are incapable.

This led Dalio to look at governance from a different perspective. Being a founder-entrepreneur, he was used to an informal system, which had no system of checks and balances. As an effect, when he stepped down from his CEO position, the transition became chaotic. Thus, there was a need to build a new governance system, which would embrace a scheme of checks and balances to keep Bridgewater afloat – even though there would be a change in the company's management.

The change to a new governance system eventually pushed through. And true enough, Dalio was able to finally step down from his temporary CEO position in April 2017.

# Looking Back from a Higher Level

From his early years, to how he successfully rebuilt Bridgewater, Dalio looks back at all his experiences with fondness and reflection. He realized that these experiences shaped him into becoming the successful man that he is today.

He notes that having good principles helped him deal with his reality. Nonetheless, he discovered most of his life and work principles by spending a lot of time reflecting. To help us save time on reflecting, Dalio pours his principles and reflections into this book's succeeding chapters.

To make it easier for readers to understand, Dalio has organized his principles in bullet form, so that distinction between higher-level principles, mid-level principles, and sub-principles wouldn't be a problem. He hopes that you will use these principles to serve as your guide towards creating meaningful work and meaningful lives.

# Embrace Reality and Deal With It

Understanding how reality works is at the heart of this principle. Keeping ourselves grounded in reality helps us analyze and deal with situations better, which eventually makes us better decision-makers.

In this chapter, Dalio encourages us to become hyperrealists. A hyperrealist is able to dream wisely, which in turn greatly increases the chances of it coming true. This principle is important because success comes from being determined to make your dreams a reality.

Nonetheless, before you can make your dreams a reality, you have to understand how reality works in the first place. The first step is to try to see things from a higher perspective. This step means taking in all the information and circumstances that can possibly affect your outcome, and try to work around them.

Another way to get in touch with reality is to be open-minded and transparent. Although none of us are born knowing the truth, we eventually discover it as we grow up. Thus, Dalio believes that if we open our minds to what others have to say, we are on the road to great success.

Also noteworthy is how we are encouraged to depend on nature and observe reality from that perspective. History tells us that man used his observations of reality in order to cope with the natural occurrences around him. This led mankind to survive for thousands of years while improving as the years went by.

Man's observations of nature and reality helped him evolve. Each person, regardless of status, is bound to evolve at different points in his life. Dalio pointed out that how we evolve also depends on how we try to stay aligned with the community – meaning, we contribute for the benefit of the whole and will be rewarded in exchange.

But perhaps the most important part of the evolutionary process is how we are able to learn from what has caused us pain. Pain is unavoidable – but if we embrace this pain and use it to improve ourselves, we are on the path toward progress. In order to have this mindset, we must not be afraid of experiencing pain – we must embrace it.

This chapter ends with Dalio reminding us to own up to our decisions. After all, the decisions we make throughout our lives will have a resulting outcome. Regardless if your decision turns out to be a mistake or an achievement, make sure to own up to it.

# Use the 5-Step Process to Get What You Want Out of Life

A person's evolutionary process takes place in five distinct steps: having clear goals, identifying and not tolerating problems, finding the root causes of problems, designing plans, and doing what's necessary to push these designs to see results. When taken together, these five steps make up a loop that ensures attainment of a person's goals. These five steps are discussed in detail below.

The first step is to have clear and defined goals. Having clear goals will help a person determine the direction that he will take in order to achieve them. To help you set clear goals, Dalio recommends that you first learn how to prioritize. As soon as you discover which goals take precedence over others, it will be easier for you to decide on what you really want to do and have in life.

The second step is identifying your problems. As you move towards achieving your goals, it is certain that you will encounter problems. Nonetheless, how you deal with these problems will determine how successful you will be in achieving your goals. Most people make the mistake of tolerating their problems – unfortunately, this only magnifies the problem. According to Dalio, the right thing to do is to view problems as a means to improve.

The third step is to get to the root causes of the problem. When you encounter problems, stay calm and keep a clear head, so that you may be analytical while dealing with them. As much as possible, try to focus on what the problem really is and determine if it is already the root cause, or if it is merely a proximate cause. Knowing this will help you hit the bulls eye and get rid of the problem completely.

In the fourth step, Dalio encourages us to design a plan that will help us get around the problem. But while doing so, keep in mind that a single plan can lead to different outcomes, and these outcomes can either be achievements or more problems. Thus, as much as possible, try to visualize and write down your design in order to avoid producing more problems.

And finally, the fifth step is to actually do something about your plan. Nothing ever comes from just dreaming about something – success follows only if you do something about that dream.

# Be Radically Open-Minded

As previously discussed, being radically open-minded helps us stay grounded in reality. Additionally, it also helps people get rid of the barriers, which stand in their way to success.

To become radically open-minded, Dalio shares that the first principle is to recognize that your ego and blind spots are your biggest barriers. And when these two work together, you fail to see yourself and your circumstances from an objective point of view. Thus, try to lower your ego and get rid of your blind spots in order to look at the world with a clear perspective.

After acknowledging our biggest barriers, the next step is to practice radical open-mindedness. This simply means that you recognize that you have barriers, so you consciously figure out ways to get past them. In effect, you end up making good decisions.

Having thoughtful disagreements with people also helps. Just like pain and mistakes, disagreements are inevitable parts of life. This is especially true if you are constantly working with people. When this happens, try to understand what they are trying to say, and where they're coming from. This gives you a bigger perspective, which will eventually help you resolve your conflicting views.

To end this chapter, Dalio shares that being open-minded is also a result of reflecting on your experiences. Among the activities, he suggested include being objective, meditating, encouraging others to be open-minded, and having faith in your decision-making process.

# Understand That People Are Wired Very Differently

People are not created equal, and knowing this fact makes it easier for you to deal with others. To help us get the right mindset, this chapter discusses the most common character traits so you can find a way to treat those with similar characteristics. □

- Right-brained and left-brained thinking. The left hemisphere of the brain is responsible for sequential reasoning, detail analysis, and especially excels at linear analysis; this makes left-brained thinkers analytically strong. On the other hand, the right hemisphere is responsible for thinking across categories, recognizing themes, and seeing the big picture; this makes right-brained thinkers street smart.

- Introversion and extroversion. Introverts are those who get their energy from ideas, memories, and experiences. On the other hand, extroverts are those who get their energy from being with people.

- Intuiting and sensing. Intuitive persons tend to prioritize context more than details, while a sensing persons focus on details.

- Thinking and feeling. Some people make logical analysis of facts and circumstances before coming up with a decision, while others rely on the harmony between people.

- Planning and perceiving. Some people prefer living in a planned and orderly way, whereas there are people who prefer living spontaneously.

- Creators, refiners, advancers, executors, and flexors. Creators are those who generate new ideas; refiners are those who challenge these ideas; advancers communicate and carry forward these ideas; executors ensure that goals are accomplished; and flexors are a combination of the previous four types.

- Tasks and goals. Some people tend to focus on daily tasks, while others prefer planning and achieving long-term tasks.

- Workplace personality inventory. According to Dalio, this is a test which helps people understand what others value.

- Shapers are those who can come up with unique visions and makes sure that they become a reality despite doubts from people. According to Dalio, this is the person you should aspire to be in order to be successful

Keeping all these traits in mind will help you improve your communication skills, which will eventually help you build meaningful relationships. It will also help you manage yourself and orchestrate others to get what you want – since you are consciously developing habits that will make doing good things habitually.

# Learn How to Make Decisions Effectively

Being a founder-entrepreneur, Dalio has lived his life as a professional decision maker. He learned how to make decisions effectively through his numerous experiences in the span of decades. Dalio shares that the key to effective decisions is by making them in a systematic and repeatable way, so that others may do the same under similar circumstances.

There is no single best way to make effective decisions. To help us improve our decision-making, Dalio lays down several rules in this chapter.

The first thing to do is to consider all the circumstances at hand. When you try to visualize the bigger picture, you begin to consider various factors, which are determinative of how successful the outcome will be.

Second, you must understand that good decision-making results from positive emotions. Having harmful emotions often creates an illusion that our problems are bigger than they really are. As a result, we not only see the bigger picture, but we end up looking at things with a tainted perspective.

Third, you must learn to weigh the value of all the information at hand. This will help you focus on deciding on more serious matters while weeding out unnecessary things.

Nonetheless, Dalio also notes that there are some decisions that we cannot make on our own. When you are having troubles with weighing out certain facts, try to get help from believable people to give you fresh insight on the matter. Alternatively, try to convert your principles into computer-based algorithms so they can make decisions for you.

# Trust in Radical Truth and Radical Transparency

Now that we're through talking about life principles, we now enter Part III of this book – work principles. Dalio shares that the first step towards forming a great work relationship is by creating an environment that cultivates trust in radical truth and radical transparency.

Radical truth means not filtering one's thoughts and questions so that issues are openly dealt with. On the other hand, radical transparency means giving everyone the ability to see everything. These two concepts are at the heart of work principles because it greatly improves how people work and interact with each other. □

In order to be radically truthful, we must first embrace the beauty of knowing the truth. Most people fear knowing the truth because it is often associated with pain and humiliation. Instead of looking at it negatively, try to look at knowing the truth as a means to improve yourself. □

For leaders, Dalio suggests creating an environment where everyone has the right to understand what makes sense. He encourages them to develop a system of meritocracy, where everyone is obliged to speak up and fight for what's right – because it helps people become more efficient in working on their tasks and contributing to the organization's overall productivity.

In order to be radically transparent, you should try to see it as a means to enforce justice. However, not all things must be available to everyone. Confidential organizational information must only be accessed by authorized individuals.

Once you have developed these traits, then you are on your road to developing meaningful work and meaningful relationships – the ultimate keys to organizational success.

# Cultivate Meaningful Work and Meaningful Relationships

Dalio lsays much emphasis must be given to meaningful relationships, since it helps in building and sustaining a culture of excellence by establishing trust and support. However, meaningful relationships can only stem from genuine interactions between people – they must not be forced into it.

Being loyal to the organization's common mission is one way to cultivate meaningful relationships. Dalio is completely against being loyal to a person, especially if he is not operating consistently with the mission. Additionally, Dalio also warns us against people who use the organization to fuel their own motives – because it only goes to show that their loyalty does not lie with the organization.

Another way to build great work relationships is to be considerate. As much as possible, try to encourage people to give consideration to others before demanding the same for themselves. This cultivates a healthy give-and-take relationship, which can greatly improve relationships.

Most importantly, try to identify the honorable people within the company and decide to keep them. These are the skilled people who will treat you well, even when you're not looking.

And finally, Dalio warns us that the size of the organization can make or break relationships. Usually, meaningful relationships breed in smaller organizations – a fact personally experienced by Dalio throughout his year with Bridgewater.

# Create a Culture in Which It Is Okay to Make Mistakes and Unacceptable Not to Learn from Them

Making mistakes is part of being human, and not something that we should be ashamed of. According to Dalio, how people see and make use of their mistakes will determine how successful they will become. You see, successful people tend to learn from their mistakes, while unsuccessful people don't.

Mistakes form part of our evolutionary process, so it is something that we should be thankful for. Unfortunately, society's glamorization of success has caused mistakes to earn a bad reputation. As much as possible, try to keep an open mind and embrace what you learned from your mistakes. After all, history is replete with successful people who rose above the pain of their mistakes and eventually lived on to become great individuals.

Additionally, some people tend to fear mistakes because they are afraid of looking bad. This is usually your ego talking.

And as previously discussed, your ego is one of the barriers that keep you from achieving your goals.

Once you've overcome your fear of making mistakes, the next step is to find a way to use them to your benefit. Dalio suggests that you write down the patterns of your mistakes so that you can avoid similar situations.

Finally, keep in mind that pain is only a mental experience. It only exists in your head, so the right way to deal with it is to reflect on it in a way that would help you grow – both as a person and as part of a community.

# Get and Stay in Sync

The success of an organization is determined by how aligned its people are on different levels. This can be a tough feat to achieve, especially since people are wired differently. Dalio instructs us that while it is difficult to do, it is certainly possible.

Conflicts can pose as a serious barrier to getting and staying in sync. However, these conflicts can also help people determine whether their principles are aligned, which eventually help resolve their differences.

The importance of resolving conflicts lies in the fact that gaps will be created within the community – something that is detrimental to any organization.

Fortunately, there are various ways to get in sync and settle conflicts. The first is to learn the art of disagreeing well. This simply means that you shouldn't hesitate on voicing out your perspective, and keeping an open mind when others voice theirs. Otherwise, disputes will be left unresolved.

Dalio also shares that keeping an open mind can help you get in sync with others. Similarly, try to acquaint yourself with people who are also open-minded and reasonable – potential people to build alignments with. And when you finally have that alignment, make sure to cherish it.

# Believability Weight Your Decision Making

According to Dalio, organizations that make the best decisions are those that embrace the culture of meritocracy with believability-weighted decision making. This kind of decision-making involves a process whereby capable people work through their disagreements with the help of capable people who are also independent thinkers.

It may seem like an intimidating thing to do, but Dalio simplifies this decision-making process with the help of the principles laid out in this chapter.

The first is to be open-minded and understand the merit behind a person's ideas. This recognizes that you can gain a bigger and deeper insight when you try to see the word from another person's eyes.

However, Dalio warns against statements beginning with "I think", because these are mere opinions that may not be backed by relevant data.

The second, and perhaps the most important principle is to find believable people who disagree with you. These people will open your eyes to other important things you might have missed. And when they do that, try to understand where they're coming from – so that you can see two sides of a story.

Nonetheless, Dalio reminds us that the disagreement must be done efficiently. If the debate seems to be going on in circles, know when to stop. Otherwise, it will only be a waste of both time and energy.

And finally, don't think that you should always get your way. Keep a fair and open mind throughout the decision-making process. Focus on the system and whether the final decision would be beneficial for the organization and the community.

# Recognize How to Get Beyond Disagreements

Also important in a system of meritocracy is the ability to get beyond disagreements. In order to attain that, Dalio points out the need to set up a path for settling disputes where concerned individuals are encouraged to fight for what they believe in.

Dalio lays emphasis on the importance of principles, for these are similar to laws that govern the organization. Additionally, these principles stem from standards of behavior, which applies to everyone. Thus, whenever a controversy is being settled, parties are required to appear with equal levels of integrity, open-mindedness, assertiveness, and consideration.

As much as possible, try to determine the conflicts that create the bigger impact, and work on resolving these first. If it seems like settlement is not an option, set up a system where people will decide on how it will be resolved, like by voting.

Having a voting system allows you to determine which side the majority picks. As a result, there will always be a small group of people who are against it. Instead of allowing this to cause a gap within the community, encourage them to open their eyes and look at the situation from a bigger perspective.

Dalio, however, recognizes the possibility of using extreme measures. But as much as possible, try to use it only when it is needed, like if it is already threatening the existence of the organization.

And finally, this principle-based way of operating is only bound to fail if the people in power refuse to operate by them. Such failure results from his personal desires – desires which have no direct and positive effect on the organization. Thus, Dalio emphasizes how important it is to choose the right people.

# Remember That the WHO Is More Important Than the WHAT

The second sub-category of Part III talks about getting the right people. People, imperfect beings as we are, are prone to making mistakes. One of these mistakes is focusing too much on what needed to be done, instead of choosing whom to give the responsibility to.

To avoid this problem, Dalio lays emphasis on choosing the right Responsible Parties (RPs). These RPs execute goals well which, in turn, guarantee excellent results. They have a clear understanding of their responsibilities and what you want them to do, so they have the capacity to run the organization at the highest levels.

Additionally, an ideal RP is always ready to face the consequences of his actions. A Responsible Party is willing to take responsibility for everything – whether it is an achievement or a failure. They do not put the blame on others, and this quality makes them great managers.

And finally, in determining who are the RPs within your organization, try to ask yourself this question: who are the people within your organization who are responsible for the results and culture which make it special? Usually, the RP works as a force that drives the team toward greatness.

# Hire Right, Because the Penalties for Hiring Wrong are Huge

Dalio emphasizes the fact that hiring is a high-risk gamble. A hiring manager only weighs out the potential candidate based on what is written on his resume and his answers on interviews. Thus, there are instances when the person hired may not always be the best fit for the job.

To avoid this expensive mishap, try to imbibe the following principles:

- Match the right person with the right job. When you design jobs, make sure that you already have a clear mental image of the qualities of your ideal employee. This will serve as your guide in assessing candidates. Factors to consider include their values, abilities, and skills.

- Try to develop a systematic and scientific means of finding the right people for the job. Additionally, Dalio warns against using one's influence in helping people to land a job – especially if he knows nothing about the job.

- Keep in mind that people are created differently, and use that to the company's advantage. Make sure to hire people who complement others and are capable of working well within a community. Also, consider the hiring process as a means for you to discover people who you would want to build strong work relationships with.

- And finally, pay close attention to a person's history. During interviews, hiring managers only rely on answers and limited behavioral hints. Thus, organizations are encouraged to perform a background check on potential employees. Try to determine their work ethic, performance, and work-related character traits.

Once you find the perfect fit, you now proceed to the issue of compensation. Keep in mind that the person you are hiring is there to make a living, so make sure to be fair to provide him with stability and opportunity. After all, being generous is more important than money – especially in the world of business.

But most importantly, you must learn to keep them by building strong and meaningful relationships with them. Usually, this process involves four processes: training, testing, evaluating, and sorting. More on this in the next chapter.

# Constantly Train, Test, Evaluate, and Sort People

Continuous evolution is necessary for an organization to stay afloat. To help employees improve, there is a need to conduct assessments in order to identify their strengths and weaknesses so that they may be properly addressed.

This process may cause pain to some people, but leaders have the responsibility and duty to maintain the organization's excellence. Nonetheless, Dalio points out that this is a process of personal evolution – something that will help them grow in the long run.

Since time immemorial, our ancestors have evolved through their experiences. Similarly, when you test people, their survivor instincts will find a way to make it through successfully. This will help you assess each person's strengths and weaknesses, and eventually determine if they are fit for their job or not.

It also helps if you continuously provide feedback based on their tests and trainings. This will help them improve their ways – just make sure to do it in an encouraging manner.

47

Dalio also points out the need to evaluate accurately. Your compliments and criticisms must be accurate and backed up by data to bolster its credibility. Sometimes, these criticisms may seem harsh, but if you remind them that it's for their own good, then it would be easier for them to swallow. After all, accurate criticisms are more valuable than shallow compliments.

Nevertheless, when a person keeps making the same mistakes despite training and evaluations, then don't hesitate to remove them. Their stay in the company is not only counterproductive – it will also build a sense of complacency within him. This also reminds others that the company only expects excellent results from them.

# Manage as Someone Operating a Machine to Achieve a Goal

Dalio says that there is a common ground among people who have goals – they set them up and build machines to achieve them. For Dalio, this machine was Bridgewater. While running Bridgewater, he would constantly compare his actual outcomes to his expected outcomes, while also finding ways to improve the machine.

In this chapter, Dalio zeroes in on high-level principles to help you build, maintain, and improve your machine or business.

Begin by looking at everything from a different point-of-view to gain insight into the situation. You can do this by comparing your outcomes vis-à-vis your goals, building great metrics, and focusing on your machine. □

Dalio also reminds you that your approach to operating your machine should have two purposes. The first is to get closer to your goal, and the second is to train and test people and your design. Since both of these factors make an ultimate impact on your machine, then it can also apply to various cases and circumstances.

Additionally, good managers are those who know their people well – what they're like and what makes them tick – and use this knowledge to improve their efficiency and ramp up their productivity. Most importantly, you should also assign responsibilities in a clear manner to avoid a potential job slip. These job slips occur when a job changes without being explicitly thought through and agreed on, which may cause the wrong people to handle the wrong responsibilities.

Also noteworthy, is knowing how to deal with key-man risk. This bolsters the fact that no person, no matter how great, is irreplaceable. Thus, a good organization must have a contingency plan wherein the key person has at least one person to become his potential successor.

Communication is also an important factor in operating your machine. All information must be clearly conveyed to avoid conflicts and errors. Additionally, Dalio suggests that each organization must have clear metrics, which would reflect and keep track of your progress.

And finally, acknowledge that you cannot do things on your own. If problems seem too tough, don't hesitate to escalate these problems – and encourage your people to do the same.

# Perceive and Don't Tolerate Problems

In every business venture, problems are inevitable. Whenever possible, try to look at problems in a positive way – like how they propel us to keep going forward. ☐

With this in mind, Dalio encourages us to see these problems as an opportunity to improve our machine. To help us get the right mindset, the following principles must be observed.

You need to worry if you aren't, and you need not worry if you are. This is due to the fact that being complacent leaves no room for improvement – because you are already satisfied with your current system. To put it in another way: if you're worried, then you don't need to worry – because your constant search to improve the system will certainly lead to success.

To help you perceive and not tolerate your problems, Dalio shares the following techniques:

• Assign people to perceive problems. Since their task zeroes in on investigating problems, they must also report their findings to independent reporting lines. This encourages them to convey problems without any fear of recrimination.

• Avoid the "Frog in the Boiling Water Syndrome". Just like the frog placed in gradually heating water, a person can get used to unacceptable things and, just like the frog, this can be detrimental to both the person and the organization in the long run. Encourage them to see things from a fresh perspective.

• Try to "taste the soup" first. Managers, like chefs, need to "taste the soup" before something goes out to the public.

• As much as possible, try to encourage people to speak up, so that communications between people will flow freely.

• When trying to address problems, try to be specific to encourage personal responsibility.

• And finally, don't be intimidated when you're fixing difficult things.

# Diagnose Problems to Get at Their Root Causes

To effectively solve a problem, your objective must be to identify the specific causes of these problems. According to Dalio, you can only do so if you know how to diagnose your problems.

In order to diagnose your problem, you have to identify: at which step did the failure occur, which principles were violated, and what you should change in order to produce better results. However, there is no hard-and-fast rule to help you determine these factors since it greatly depends on the situation.

It is also important to understand that diagnosing your problems isn't a one-time activity. As much as possible, try to do it continuously so that you will always find ways to improve. More specifically, Dalio makes special mention of the "drill-down" technique – a 4-step process involving the listing down of problems, identifying the root causes, creating a plan, and executing the plan. Although a drill-down is not really a diagnosis, it can greatly help you gain an understanding of the root cause of any problem.

And finally, we must keep in mind that this process is necessary for the organizations foundational progress. By getting to the root of the problem, you are opening the doors to upgrading the working systems, while also building quality relationships.

# Design Improvements to Your Machine to Get Around Your Problems

After successfully diagnosing your problems, the next step is to design your machine in a way that would make it solve these problems. For Bridgewater, this stage was implemented by their Client Service Department, which was responsible for designing and implementing changes after receiving results of their diagnosis.

Nonetheless, Dalio also emphasizes the importance of reflecting on these problems, so that each member can see the bigger picture. The following principles will help you in designing your machine – and how to do it well.

The first principle is to build your machine. While doing so, observe what you're doing, why you're doing it, and consider the circumstances surrounding the cases at hand to come up with relevant work principles.

While building your machine, make sure to center it around your goals rather than merely being tasks. Tasks are things you need to do within a short period of time, while goals are more long-term. Thus, this helps you focus and prioritize the matters which require immediate attention. Build your organization from the top down.⬜

Dalio also encourages us to create an organizational chart. However, this must look like a pyramid with lines that don't cross – this means that people should focus working only on matters that concern their department. This also means clearly delineating a person's responsibilities and setting up reporting lines in case unexpected events. To attain this, you can seek help from "leveragers" – people who are capable of going from conceptual to practical in an effective manner, while also making sure that concepts get implemented.

Nonetheless, Dalio reminds us to never let go of our strategic vision. But while our overall vision remains constant, we must tweak it by adding the necessary and appropriate changes to adjust to different circumstances.

# Do What You Set Out to Do

The final step of the 5-Step Process requires you to do what you have to do. After all, conceptualization is nothing if you don't do anything about it. However, getting started is also the hardest step.

To nudge his readers to take the first step, Dalio suggests that you should only work on goals that you are excited about. As much as possible, try to think of various ways in which you can make your tasks align and connect with those goals so that you wouldn't feel burdened by them. Most importantly, try to think things through before acting on them to increase your efficiency.

There is also a need for us to recognize that all of us have a lot on our plate. Sometimes, we feel frustrated because it seems that we have more responsibilities than others when in fact, we have equal amount of work – the difference lies in how calmly they deal with these responsibilities.

Dalio also suggests that we try to maintain a checklist. This checklist will serve as a reminder of the tasks that we have to do, while also confirming which ones are already been done.

Sometimes, what keeps us from trying is our fear of failures. Dalio shares that this quote from Winston Churchill has kept him going amidst his many failures, and he hopes that it could help us, too: "Success consists of going from failure to failure without loss of enthusiasm."

Nonetheless, working without taking time to rest is highly discouraged. Always build downtimes between working – otherwise, you will end up suffering from a burnout. And when you have finally achieved your goals, find time to celebrate this milestone.

# Use Tools and Protocols to Shape How Work Is Done

Dalio understands that being able to do something is different from wanting to do something. Thus, he encourages us to use tools and other means so that getting the work done becomes easier to do.

Similarly, the principles laid down in this book are not simply here to inspire you to make the change – instead, they are here so that you can actually make the change. In order to do so, tools must be used in a way that would promote these principles.

These tools can benefit an organization in different ways. The first is to use it as a means for internal and habitual learning in order to inspire positive behavioral change. Usually, these habitual learnings teach employees to be more efficient, while leaders learn to address problems better – thus resulting in an overall improvement.

Organizations also use these tools to create and inspire an environment of fairness and confidence. It must be noted that some organizational tools keep track of data, which can be assessed to come up with conclusions, and solutions that can impact how the organization works.

Thus, the success of an organization is not only dependent on great leaders and skillful workers – tools, equipment, and similar systems are equally essential.

# And for Heaven's Sake, Don't Overlook Governance!

At this point, you are now informed of the secrets to maintaining meaningful work and a meaningful life. However, all these principles are useless if you don't have a good governance system to tie them all together.

Governance refers to the process that checks and balances power to ensure that the interests of the community are placed above individual interests. Under this chapter, Dalio keeps emphasizing the importance of giving this power to capable people who have the right values and are able to do their jobs well. The following factors are to be considered:

- Since all organizations are required to have checks and balances, a good leader must be weighed based on his merits, responsibility, and authority. Merit alone will not suffice if he lacks in other aspects of leadership. ☐

- Understand that no person – even if he is at the top of the corporate ladder – is irreplaceable. Always keep in mind that the system is always more powerful than any person.

- People who will be given leadership responsibilities will have access to confidential information, so try to look for leaders who are trustworthy enough to keep your company's secrets.

From his personal experience, Dalio advises organizations to have many equally great leaders than just having one great leader. Additionally, when an organization depends too much on one person, it creates several problems, like producing key-man risk, limiting the range of expertise, and failing to establish adequate checks and balances.

And finally, great partnership is at the heart of successful governance systems. Within any organization, it is the glue that holds all principles, rules, and checks and balances together.

# Conclusion

Our principles guide us throughout life. In fact, how we deal with reality, make our decisions, and achieve our goals greatly depend on the principles we have formed. Nonetheless, we do not develop these principles overnight – it requires a process of trial, error, reflection, and correction. And more often than not, it can take decades before we can come up with a set of principles to live by.

Fortunately, Dalio has lived long enough to share his life and work principles with us. Being the founder-entrepreneur of Bridgewater, one of the most notable investment management firms across the globe, Dalio surely has enough experiences to share – and for us to learn from.

To bolster his credibility, Dalio shares his life story in the first part of this book. He narrates how, at the tender age of twelve, he began to take interest in the stock market. Unknown to him at that time, this first step would propel him to become one of the greatest shapers of his time.

With his limited knowledge of the stock market, however, Dalio failed to see the looming problems ahead. This caused him to experience a market crash for the first time. Nonetheless, it didn't stop him from learning more about investing – and this time, he began to spread his wings to other markets like livestock and commodities.

Right after graduating from Harvard Business School, he immediately set up Bridgewater. And within a span of forty years, the company has experienced extreme lows before it was able to achieve the reputation that it has today.

For Dalio, these extreme lows led him to discover important life and work principles which can be applied by everyone – regardless of where they are in life, and what they are working on. And for this reason, this book was born.

In the second part of this book, Dalio lays down his life principles in five chapters. These five chapters taught us that in order to successfully deal with reality, we have to fully embrace it. Dalio also lays down the steps we have to do in order to achieve what we want: having goals, not tolerating problems, diagnosing problems, designing a plan to resolve problems, and doing what's necessary to attain results.

The last part of this book lays down the work principles that Dalio has developed through the course of his forty-year journey with Bridgewater. He divides this part into three subcategories. The first sub-category inspires us to get the culture right by encouraging people to be truthful, transparent, and not be afraid of making mistakes. Also of equal importance is the capacity to cultivate meaningful work and meaningful relationships, which can help people get in sync to perform better, make better decisions, and get beyond disagreements.

On the other hand, the second sub-category teaches us how we can the right people to do the right job. Here, Dalio reminds us that hiring the wrong people can be costly and that maintaining an excellent business requires constant training, testing, evaluating, and sorting of people.

And finally, the third sub-category lays down the things we have to do in order to help the organization prosper. Usually, this means that we have to keep evolving and upgrading how we do things in order to work around its problems. Nonetheless, there will always be a need to maintain a system of checks and balances to guarantee long-term success.

# FREE BONUSES

### P.S. Is it okay if we overdeliver?

Here at Readtrepreneur Publishing, we believe in overdelivering way beyond our reader's expectations. Is it okay if we overdeliver?

Here's the deal, we're going to give you an extremely condensed PDF summary of the book which you've just read and much more...

What's the catch? We need to trust you... You see, we want to overdeliver and in order for us to do that, we've to trust our reader to keep this bonus a secret to themselves? Why? Because we don't want people to be getting our exclusive PDF summaries even without buying our books itself. Unethical, right?

Ok. Are you ready?

Firstly, remember that your book is code: "**READ67**".

Next, visit this link: **http://bit.ly/exclusivepdfs**

Everything else will be self explanatory after you've visited: **http://bit.ly/exclusivepdfs**.

We hope you'll enjoy our free bonuses as much as we enjoyed preparing it for you!